COURAGE AND GROWTH

BY JIM OLLHOFF

Printed in the United States of America, North Mankato, Minnesota.
112010
012011

 PRINTED ON RECYCLED PAPER

Editor: John Hamilton
Graphic Design: John Hamilton
Cover Design: Neil Klinepier
Cover Photo: Getty Images
Interior Photos and Illustrations: Corbis-pgs 6-7, 26-27; Getty Images-pgs 4-5, 7, 10-11, 12, 13, 14-15, 16-17, 18, 19, 20-21, 23, 24, 25; ThinkStock-pgs 8-9, 28-29.

Library of Congress Cataloging-in-Publication Data

Ollhoff, Jim, 1959-
  Courage and growth / Jim Ollhoff.
    p. cm. -- (African-American history)
  Includes index.
  ISBN 978-1-61714-711-1
  1. African Americans--Civil rights--History--20th century--Juvenile literature. 2. Civil rights movements--United States--History--20th century--Juvenile literature. 3. African Americans--Social conditions--20th century--Juvenile literature. 4. African Americans--Politics and government--Juvenile literature. 5. United States--Race relations--Juvenile literature. I. Title.
  E185.61.O374 2011
  323.1196'073--dc22
                    2010038370

CONTENTS

The Civil Rights Struggle 4

The Civil Rights Act & Affirmative Action 8

Freedom Summer and Bloody Sunday 10

The Death of Martin Luther King Jr................................14

Continued Steps Forward..16

Steps Backward..20

New African American Voices 22

The First African American President...............................26

Continued Courage and Growth..28

Glossary..30

Index 32

THE CIVIL RIGHTS STRUGGLE

The civil rights movement was a fight for basic human rights.

Historians sometimes talk about the civil rights decade, from 1954 to 1964. It was filled with intense activities and events that affected civil rights, especially for African Americans. However, the fight for civil rights started long before 1954, and continues to this day. The civil rights movement has always been led by people who stand up for what's right. It's about individuals who break through walls and boundaries.

Sometimes, an advance in civil rights happens because of a terrible tragedy that unites people behind a cause. This very thing happened in a bombing on September 15, 1963. A bomb exploded at an African American church in Birmingham, Alabama, on Sunday morning. The Sixteenth Street Baptist Church was a meeting place for civil rights activists. The bomb was planted by Ku Klux Klan members who wanted to disrupt civil rights progress. The bombing killed four young girls who were attending Sunday school. This senseless act of terror shook the nation, and further united people pushing for civil rights.

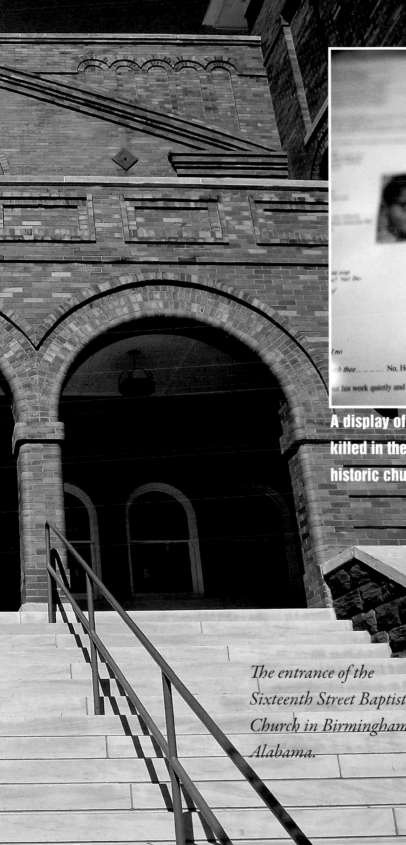

A display of photos of the four girls killed in the 1963 bombing at the historic church.

The entrance of the Sixteenth Street Baptist Church in Birmingham, Alabama.

5

A blow to the civil rights movement happened in 1963. President John F. Kennedy had been actively working for civil rights laws. But on November 22, 1963, while President Kennedy was visiting Dallas, Texas, he was killed by an assassin's bullet.

Vice President Lyndon Johnson immediately took over as president. Johnson was from Texas, and was not expected to fight vigorously for civil rights. However, he surprised many people by continuing to press for civil rights legislation.

In early 1964, the Twenty-Fourth Amendment to the United States Constitution was ratified, or put into law. The process began during the Kennedy Administration, but it became law when Lyndon Johnson was president. This amendment eliminated a practice called the poll tax. This was a fee charged to people who voted in many Southern states. The tax made it difficult for poor people, especially African Americans, to vote. Poll taxes were put in place after the Civil War, when African Americans were given the right to vote. The Twenty-Fourth Amendment made poll taxes illegal.

President Kennedy in Dallas, Texas, minutes before he was assassinated.

Vice President Lyndon Johnson takes the oath of office aboard Air Force One following the death of President Kennedy.

THE CIVIL RIGHTS ACT & AFFIRMATIVE ACTION

In 1964, President Johnson signed the Civil Rights Act. This was a huge collection of laws with far-reaching changes. The Civil Rights Act of 1964 enforced the desegregation of public schools. The act made it illegal to show racial discrimination or bias in interstate business. It took away federal funding from schools that endorsed discrimination. It made voter registration equal, instead of white voters being treated differently than black voters.

President Johnson said that civil rights laws by themselves weren't enough to stop discrimination. In September 1965, the president issued Executive Order 11246. It required government-assisted businesses to take "affirmative action" toward minority employees. Businesses getting funding from the government had to make a plan to hire minorities, and make sure they were treated the same as white workers. The executive order made it illegal to not hire someone simply because they were black.

W. Robertson

DI399

FREEDOM SUMMER AND BLOODY SUNDAY

In the summer of 1964, a civil rights group called the Student Nonviolent Coordinating Committee (SNCC) decided on its next goal: to register African Americans so they could vote. They called it "Freedom Summer." The SNCC decided to work in Mississippi, a place that still had many segregationists. White and black volunteers, mostly college students, poured into Mississippi. Most of the volunteers expected to be arrested for their actions. Three were murdered by Ku Klux Klan members.

Despite the risks and tragedies, huge numbers of African Americans became registered to vote. Before Freedom Summer, only seven percent of African Americans in Mississippi were registered to vote. After the Freedom Summer campaign, 67 percent were registered to vote.

Hundreds of children and teens from New York and Philadelphia, Pennsylvania, rally July 14, 2004, to celebrate the 40th anniversary of Freedom Summer, the 1964 voter registration drive that targeted African Americans in Mississippi.

Martin Luther King Jr. (center) leads a group of civil rights demonstrators on the road from Selma, Alabama, to the state capital of Montgomery.

A few months later, in Selma, Alabama, Martin Luther King Jr. led peaceful protest marches to encourage voter registration. The authorities had banned protests, fearing that violence would result, but King and his followers ignored the order. On March 7, 1965, about 600 civil rights marchers were attacked by state police with clubs, whips, and tear gas. The events were captured by the news media and broadcast to a shocked nation. The day was called Bloody Sunday, and it helped unite the nation to push for civil rights.

Today, the route taken by the marchers is a National Historic Trail. It is called the Selma to Montgomery Voting Rights Trail.

An aerial view showing a long column of civil rights demonstrators, led by Dr. Martin Luther King Jr., on March 21, 1965, as they cross a bridge in Selma, Alabama. This third and final march made it to the state capital of Montgomery, 51 miles (82 km) away.

THE DEATH OF MARTIN LUTHER KING JR.

One of the most important leaders in history was Martin Luther King Jr. Born in 1929, he went to school to become a pastor, but he also became the leader of the civil rights movement. His vision for a world transformed by peace and nonviolence continues to inspire people today.

In a terrible blow to the civil rights movement, Martin Luther King Jr. was killed on April 4, 1968. He was standing on the balcony of his Memphis, Tennessee, hotel room when he was shot. Despite emergency surgery, he was pronounced dead at the hospital.

Word of King's death quickly spread. Driven by grief and anger, riots broke out in cities across the United States. Leaders pleaded for calm, citing Martin Luther King's mission of nonviolence.

About two months after the shooting, suspect James Earl Ray was arrested at Heathrow Airport in London, England. He was transported back to Tennessee, where he was given a 99-year prison sentence for King's murder.

Civil rights leader Andrew Young (left) and others on the balcony of the Lorraine Motel in Memphis, Tennessee, pointing in the direction of gunshots after the assassination of civil rights leader Martin Luther King Jr., who is lying at their feet.

CONTINUED STEPS FORWARD

Presidential candidate Reverend Jesse Jackson raising linked hands with civil rights pioneer Rosa Parks during the Democratic National Convention, July 19, 1988, in Atlanta, Georgia.

In 1968, President Johnson signed another Civil Rights Act. The 1968 act prevented discrimination based on race, religion, or national origin in the buying or renting of houses. No longer could Americans be denied a home simply because they were black.

The 1970s and the following years showed continued steps forward for civil rights. In the political world, more and more African Americans were elected as mayors, congressional representatives, and senators. In 1984 and 1988, civil rights activist Jesse Jackson became a serious contender in the presidential race.

African Americans made gains economically, too. Starting in the 1960s, black-owned businesses increased significantly. Many more African Americans were able to attend college so that they could get better jobs.

Shirley Chisholm was the first African American woman elected to Congress.

Shirley Chisholm (1924-2005)

Born in Brooklyn, New York, to immigrant parents, Shirley Chisholm became the first African American woman elected to the United States Congress in Washington, DC. She represented New York's 12th Congressional District as a Democrat from 1969 to 1983. In 1972, she ran for president of the United States. She was the first African American from a major political party to run for the presidency. Before becoming a congresswoman, she was a teacher. In her careers before and after serving in Congress, she always worked to end racism and sexism.

Colin Powell was the first African American to serve as secretary of state.

Colin Powell (1937-)

American statesman Colin Powell served the United States in a number of different positions. He was born in New York City. His immigrant parents were from Jamaica. He joined the U.S. Army and rose through the ranks, with service during the war in Vietnam. He became a four-star general. He served as national security advisor and as chairman of the Joint Chiefs of Staff. In 2001, Powell became President George W. Bush's secretary of state, the highest-ranking member of the president's cabinet. As secretary of state, it was Powell's job to oversee America's relations with other countries. Colin Powell was the first African American to serve in that position.

STEPS BACKWARD

There were many gains in the last half of the twentieth century for the African American community. However, there were steps backward as well.

One of the steps backward was the explosion of drug abuse. In the 1980s and 1990s, crack cocaine became a popular drug. It was highly addictive, and it hit the African American community especially hard. With drugs came drug dealers, and with drug dealers came gang violence. All these things led to unemployment, murders, crime, and hopelessness for many people.

In 1991, several Los Angeles, California, police officers were caught on video beating Rodney King, an African American who had been arrested after a high-speed car chase. When a jury found the police officers not guilty of using excessive force, rioting exploded in Los Angeles. The incident is evidence that racial tension continues to simmer in the United States.

Since the 1990s, African American leaders have created many successful programs to reduce crime. However, problems such as drug use and gang violence remain high in many communities. Also, young black men have a higher rate of being sent to jail than whites or other racial groups who are accused of similar crimes. Some say this is evidence of racism in the courts. Others say it is proof of continued poverty among the black community.

NEW AFRICAN AMERICAN VOICES

In the last half of the twentieth century and the first part of this century, African Americans continued to break through racial barriers. Cultural movements emerged that better showed the identity of the black community, and gave it a more effective voice.

Hip-hop music emerged out of New York City in the 1970s. By the 1990s, it had become very popular worldwide. Some rap music lyrics addressed the poverty that was still a problem for many in the black community. Early superstars included Public Enemy, known for their politically charged lyrics, and Run-D.M.C., a group that helped bring mainstream acceptance to hip-hop music. Innovations in hip-hop continue to make it a popular style of music today.

Actor Sidney Poitier became a box-office star with classic films such as *In the Heat of the Night* and *Guess Who's Coming to Dinner*. In television, Bill Cosby starred in *I Spy* in the 1960s. He was one of the first black actors to star in a weekly show. The science-fiction show *Star Trek* featured black actress Nichelle Nichols as an officer aboard the starship *Enterprise*. In the 1980s, Bill Cosby returned to television with *The Cosby Show*. It was extremely popular with both white and black audiences.

Run-D.M.C.

Sidney Poitier

Nichelle Nichols

Bill Cosby

23

Michael Jordan

Maya Angelou

Sports of all kinds helped showcase the talents of black athletes. In 1947, Jackie Robinson became the first black American to play in modern Major League Baseball. He played for the Brooklyn Dodgers. His courage and determination made it possible for others to follow. Since then, African Americans have been well represented in most professional sports. Superstars include football's Walter Payton, basketball's Michael Jordan, and golf's Tiger Woods.

African Americans became great writers, as well. Maya Angelou, a remarkable poet, recited "On the Pulse of Morning" at President Bill Clinton's inauguration in 1993. She is perhaps most famous for her autobiography, *I Know Why the Caged Bird Sings*.

Recent immigration from other African countries, such as Somalia, has increased in the United States. This has provided even more voices for the rich diversity of African American culture.

In 1999, *Sports Illustrated* magazine declared boxer Muhammad Ali "Sportsman of the Century."

Muhammad Ali (1942-)

Many sports fans consider Muhammad Ali to be the greatest boxer of all time. He was born Cassius Clay in Louisville, Kentucky. After winning several Golden Gloves titles, in 1960 he won a gold medal at the Summer Olympic Games in Rome, Italy. In 1964, he revealed that he was a member of the Nation of Islam, an African American activist religious group, and that he had changed his name to Muhammad Ali.

During his long and successful professional boxing career, Ali won 56 matches, losing only five. He was a three-time World Heavyweight Champion. He competed in many famous fights, including several with his rivals Joe Frazier and George Foreman. Muhammad Ali's nickname was "The Greatest."

Ali had a showy personality and an unorthodox fighting style. When he described his fighting style, he sometimes said he would "float like a butterfly, sting like a bee." In 1999, *Sports Illustrated* magazine declared Muhammad Ali "Sportsman of the Century."

THE FIRST
AFRICAN
AMERICAN
PRESIDENT

On January 20, 2009, Barack Obama was sworn in as the 44th president of the United States. He won a landslide victory over his Republican opponent, John McCain. As the first African American president, Obama became a symbol to many people that the worst years of racism were behind us.

President Obama was born in Hawaii in 1961. His father, also named Barack, was born in Kenya, Africa. His white mother was born in Kansas, but lived in Hawaii as an adult. President Obama's parents met at the University of Hawaii.

Barack Obama worked himself through college and law school, and eventually moved to Chicago, Illinois. He worked to help communities there rebuild after some major employers shut down. He became an expert on constitutional law, and taught that subject at the University of Chicago. He became a state senator in Illinois, and then a United States senator. He and his wife, Michelle, have two children, Malia and Sasha.

CONTINUED COURAGE AND GROWTH

History is full of times of terrible violence and cruelty. However, people often rose up against injustice, and great leaders emerged. During the years of slavery, hope came from people like Harriet Tubman and Frederick Douglass. During the civil rights era, leaders like Martin Luther King Jr. gave people courage.

Will racism ever end? Unfortunately, there has always been hate, ignorance, and fear, and there probably always will be. The African American journey began with slavery in the 1500s. Today, most African Americans know a measure of freedom and equality that their ancestors could only dream of. Still, humanity has a long way to go before racism and bigotry can be stamped out forever.

Today, people of every skin color, every religion, and every nation continue pushing to make Martin Luther King's vision a reality: *"I have a dream my four little children will one day live in a nation where they will not be judged by the color of their skin but by the content of their character."*

GLOSSARY

Civil Rights

The rights of all individuals to participate equally in their communities.

Civil War

The war fought between America's Northern and Southern states from 1861–1865. The Southern states were for slavery. They wanted to start their own country. Northern states fought against slavery and a division of the country.

Constitutional Law

Law that deals with how governments create and use their power. Most governments have written constitutions, which explain how laws are to be carried out. Constitutions are usually very complicated. People going to school to become lawyers can specialize in studying constitutional law.

Desegregation

Integrating black people and white people into the same facility, school, or place of business. After desegregation laws were passed, there could no longer be "whites only" facilities. Desegregation ended the forced separation of blacks and whites.

Inauguration

A ceremony in which a person who wins an election officially takes office.

Joint Chiefs of Staff

Military leaders who advise the president and other civilian leaders of the United States. They include a member from each of the four branches of the military—the Army, Air Force, Navy, and Marines—plus a chairman and vice chairman appointed by the president. Colin Powell was the first African American to serve as chairman of the Joint Chiefs of Staff. He was appointed by President George H.W. Bush in 1989. As chairman, he oversaw several military crises, including Operation Desert Storm during the 1991 Persian Gulf War.

Ku Klux Klan

Often referred to as the KKK, the Ku Klux Klan is an extreme, racist organization that believes in the supremacy of white people over all others. It was formed in the Southern states after the Civil War. The group used violence to oppose equal rights for African Americans. Ku Klux Klan members often disguised themselves by dressing in white robes with hoods, and burned wooden crosses as a Klan symbol. The Ku Klux Klan still exists today, with independent chapters across the country, with most in the Southern United States.

Racism

The belief that people of one skin color are better than a people of another skin color; or, that individuals of a certain skin color have certain characteristics *because* of their skin color.

Segregation

The practice of separating blacks and whites. A segregated school, for example, could only have either white children or black children.

INDEX

A

Ali, Muhammad 25
Angelou, Maya 24
Army, U.S. 19

B

Birmingham, AL 4
Bloody Sunday 12
Brooklyn, NY 18
Brooklyn Dodgers 24
Bush, George W. 19

C

Chicago, IL 27
Chisholm, Shirley 18
Civil Rights Act of 1964 8
Civil Rights Act of 1968 17
Civil War 6
Clay, Cassius 25
Clinton, Bill 24
Congress, U.S. 18
Constitution, U.S. 6
Cosby, Bill 22
Cosby Show, The 22

D

Dallas, TX 6
Douglass, Frederick 28

E

Enterprise 22
Executive Order 11246 8

F

Foreman, George 25
Frazier, Joe 25
Freedom Summer 10

G

Golden Gloves 25
Guess Who's Coming to Dinner 22

H

Hawaii 27
Heathrow Airport 14

I

I Know Why the Caged Bird Sings 24
I Spy 22
Illinois 27
In the Heat of the Night 22

J

Jackson, Jesse 17
Jamaica 19
Johnson, Lyndon 6, 8, 17
Joint Chiefs of Staff 19
Jordon, Michael 24

K

Kansas 27
Kennedy, John F. 6
Kenya 27
King, Martin Luther, Jr. 12, 14, 28
King, Rodney 20
Ku Klux Klan 4, 10

L

London, England 14
Los Angeles, CA 20
Louisville, KY 25

M

Major League Baseball 24
McCain, John 27
Memphis, TN 14
Mississippi 10

N

Nation of Islam 25
New York, NY 18, 19, 22
Nichols, Nichelle 22

O

Obama, Barack 27
Obama, Malia 27
Obama, Michelle 27
Obama, Sasha 27
Olympic Games, Summer 25
"On the Pulse of Morning" 24

P

Payton, Walter 24
Poitier, Sidney 22
Powell, Colin 19
Public Enemy 22

R

Ray, James Earl 14
Robinson, Jackie 24
Rome, Italy 25
Run-D.M.C. 22

S

Selma, AL 12
Selma to Montgomery Voting Rights Trail 12
Sixteenth Street Baptist Church 4
Somalia 24
Sports Illustrated 25
Star Trek 22
Student Nonviolent Coordinating Committee (SNCC) 10

T

Texas 6
Tubman, Harriet 28
12th Congressional District (New York) 18
Twenty-Fourth Amendment 6

U

United States 6, 14, 18, 19, 20, 24, 27
University of Chicago 27
University of Hawaii 27

V

Vietnam 19

W

Washington, DC 18
Woods, Tiger 24
World Heavyweight Championship 25